When Cancer Comes Your Way
A Couple's Guide To
Finding Hope & Keeping The Faith

*To Jeremy
Future PA
Good luck,
Howard Clarke*

Other Resources by Howard F. Clarke

"Divine Dialogue: 50 Familiar Phrases from the Bible & the Stories Behind Them"

Available From
Amazon.com (Trade Paperback)
And
www.ebookmall.com (ebook version)

When Cancer Comes Your Way

A Couple's Guide To Finding Hope & Keeping The Faith

By

Howard F. Clarke & Beverley Clarke

When Cancer Comes Your Way:
A Couple's Guide To Finding Hope &
Keeping the Faith

Copyright © 2009 Howard F. Clarke

ISBN 1440486328

All rights reserved. No portion of this book may be reproduced, stored in a retrieval system, or transmitted in any form or by any means – electronic, mechanical, photocopy, recording, scanning, or other – except for brief quotations in critical reviews or articles, without the prior written permission of the author.

1st Trade Paperback Edition
Printed 2009 by CreateSpace, an Amazon.com Company

Bible Quotations, The Authorized King James Version

*I have fought a good fight,
I have finished my course,
I have kept the faith."*

2 Timothy 4:7

To Our Fellow Travelers and Their Companions

CONTENTS

Preface   9

Prologue: "Green Chair Thoughts"   11

Chapter 1 "First Signs"   17

Chapter 2 "Trials and Thanksgivings"   23

Chapter 3 "Diagnosis"   33

Chapter 4 "Journey Preparations"   41

Chapter 5 "Surgery and the Soul"   57

Chapter 6 "Chemo"   79

Chapter 7 "No Piece of Cake"   93

CONTENTS (continued)

Chapter 8 "The Long Haul"   **99**

Chapter 9 "Crisis Mode"   **117**

Chapter 10 "Reprieve"   **129**

Afterword   **135**

Appendix A   **141**
Quick Reference: Survival Tips

Appendix B   **145**
Neutropenic Diet & Precautions

Appendix C   **147**
Helpful Resources

About The Authors   **149**

Preface

Cancer is a harsh word. It is a harsh word, but *not* an immediate death sentence.

That is the first and most important lesson.

The cancer journey is a tough one, very demanding with twists and turns and detours. A hopeful attitude, the right support, and some practical knowledge about potential pitfalls are extremely important. Even more important is an abiding faith.

This book contains an honest look at one cancer journey as told through the eyes and perspectives of caregiver and patient and contains what we believe are helpful lessons we have learned along the way.

At the beginning of each chapter are excerpts from my wife's journal in her role of caregiver, while the bulk of the book is based upon my recollections and observances as a cancer patient.

This book is about adults and for adults, though some of the encounters we had may apply to younger patients. I have no experience in childhood cancers, neither as a medical provider, nor as a cancer patient. Some references are offered in the Appendices for help in this difficult area.

A "Lessons Learned" section follows the end of each chapter and there is a Quick Reference at the back of the book. Please keep in mind that these suggestions are second to your own physician's advice.

We hope this book encourages the cancer patient to "keep the faith" and the caregiver to keep caring without feeling overwhelmed, discouraged, or alone.

– Howard Clarke,
Fort Worth, Texas,
April 2009

Prologue: *Green Chair Thoughts*

On that first chemo day, I asked Linda, the supervising nurse, "How likely is it that my hair *won't* fall out?"

"Mm, about a one percent chance," she said.

"Maybe I'll be that one percent," I said, grinning. I had grabbed me a good green chair. My first triumph.

But she just smiled back and shrugged. "You never know."

On the oncology floor, the first thing every patient quickly learns is to find a good chair. By "good," I mean close to the restroom, yet not jammed in among the other chairs.

You know, like living in the suburb: close to amenities, but not too close.

The chairs were green and reclinable. Blankets were plentiful, but everyone gets cold during chemo and a wise patient wants one of those really soft, fuzzy blankets they had there.

"..another skill for survival..."

So you learn to go after one of these blankets as soon as you arrive…as soon as you secure a prime green chair, that is.

(My wife thinks it's just another form of unending competition with me, i.e., see if I can grab the best, most advantageous chair and a good blanket before the other guy—or gal.) Okay, maybe I do compete a bit too much, but Life's a game, after all. Isn't it? No? Okay, maybe not. But making a game of things is another skill for survival.

And I don't bowl anyone over; if someone beats me to a chair or blanket, they are welcome. It's just a mental game, after all. In fact, I've given up my blanket to folks who need it more. Honest.

The chemo floor was a long open bay, separated into sections by big bookcases, and illuminated by a wall-to-wall picture window with a great view of bushes and trees and, I would swear, the same mockingbird hopping around out there each time I came.

Suspended over us patients was a jungle canopy of dangling IV lines, every line connecting to one of us with a clear plastic bag filled with fluid—mostly clear fluid, but sometimes yellow or red.

Red. I would soon became intimately acquainted with "Red" or "Red Man," a chemo agent officially known as Adriamycin, a powerful drug that, I was warned, would turn my tears and urine into a bright crimson.

A few minutes ago, my pre-chemo IV was started—a gentle concoction of Benadryl and anti-nausea medicine—and I finally convinced Bev, my wife, that I would be fine.

Bev departed reluctantly, looking back at me just as she turned the corner.

"It must be hard to leave your spouse there and walk away..."

I think it must be hard to leave your spouse there and walk away, but they don't provide family chairs on the floor; there was no room. There was a large lobby outside, but there would be no sense in family waiting there all day. No one did, unless there were extreme circumstances or the family had travelled many miles to be there.

A chaplain, looking somewhat military in his short haircut and neat clothes, crouched down beside my recliner.

His own wife was a cancer patient, he told me, and I could imagine that his situation provided him great empathy and spiritual sensitivity toward the other patients.

I also imagined that he struggled with his own fears and concerns for his wife, no matter how spiritual a man he might be. We talked a while and he moved on to minister to others.

I looked around to survey the other patients, mostly older folks, many of them with their heads wrapped in bandanas or covered with baseball caps. One of them was watching me from his own green chair a few feet away.

"What are you in for?"

The patient, an elderly fellow with his head clearly bald under his worn Dallas Cowboys cap, nodded hello and asked me, as if I were a cellmate and not a patient, "What are you in for?"

And, as I started to answer him, I thought back to how this journey began…how I ended up on a green chair.

Chapter 1: *First Signs*

I was called into Howard's room at about 1:00 a.m. and he seemed, finally, to be resting pain-free. The attending physician (a young woman) came in right behind me.

The physician, with no compassion or hesitation, said Howard had a lesion on his liver from "metastases," which, to my mind, meant Howard had cancer that had spread. It took me by surprise and for several moments, I really couldn't grasp anything else the doctor had to say; I could only find myself rejecting her harsh, clinical tone—a tone that brought unwanted memories and feelings surging back from years before.

I was looking at my husband lying there on the ER gurney and remembering my mother who, years before, battled liver cancer and fought to live while doctors and nurses would tell us "we don't want to give you false hope." But hope is an amazing thing and I wanted it even if they were unwilling to give it, even if, in their eyes, it was a false hope.

"Hope is an amazing thing and I wanted it even if they were unwilling to give it…"

An old saying came to mind: "Man proposes, but God disposes." I knew who my hope was in and, this time, I would let Him decide. – From Beverley's Journal

When the word "cancer" is thrown at you, your world tends to stop cold.

The lives of everyone around you go on—but not yours. Your aspirations suddenly seem pale, your future remote, your world constricted, as if you were a mouse trapped under a box with nowhere to run…until someone decides to lift the box.

At least, that's how it felt to me that night, back in November 2006.

I was stretched out on an Emergency Room gurney and waiting to learn the results of an abdominal ultrasound when the young ER doc showed up in her clean, crisp lab coat and bluntly announced, "It looks like you have metastases."

So, as bad as the word "cancer" might be, there was one that was even worse.

"Metastases?" I asked. "From where?" My prostate? Colon? I took a mental survey of my own body and came up negative.

"I remember having an unnatural calmness..."

Yet, I remember having an unnatural calmness about that entire preposterous conversation. Some might attribute that to me being medicated for pain, but that would be disallowing the prayers that Bev, outside in the waiting room, would have been pouring over me.

Bev would be in prayer, I had no doubt.

"Metastases?" I asked again. Maybe I heard wrong.

"On the ultrasound, it looks like you have a couple lesions in the liver with the typical appearance of metastases," the ER doctor said.

Did she know I was in the medical field? She must have.

No one would treat a nonmedical person—a patient with no medical knowledge—this way. This unsympathetically. God help me from ever being this harsh with my own patients.

"We can release you," she was saying, "and try to control your pain, while you get this worked up as an outpatient or we can put you in the hospital and continue tests here."

I opted for admission. Get it over with, I thought. I broke the news to Bev and she took it like a trooper, never letting on how much she must have been worried.

Bev, after I was admitted to the hospital, went home to make phone calls to the family and to tend to our dog, Daisy. I tried to mentally prepare myself for the liver biopsy that was coming (I had two biopsies; the first inconclusive.) All this after what I thought was a simple gallbladder attack. Life comes at you from all directions, I thought morosely. Let the games begin.

Lessons Learned

1. Cancer is a powerfully negative force. It naturally becomes the top priority—after God and your family—in your life. But it does not define who you are.
2. Hang onto hope—even if others try to steal it. In the end, your hope lies beyond earthly rules and controls.
3. Don't underestimate the power of prayer. It has an unnatural—supernatural—calming effect (the "peace that passes understanding...")
4. Don't accept quick judgments about your condition and prognosis, especially when they are negative. The classically pessimistic "you only have six months to live" statement has often been proven wrong by patients refusing to give up without a fight.
5. God is in control.

Chapter 2: *Trials and Thanksgivings*

I came home alone and had a good cry. This upset our dog, a yellow Lab named Daisy, who stayed close by my side until she finally got too tired to keep her eyes open and crawled into her kennel bed to sleep. It was very late—actually, it was very early in the morning. I called our church prayer line and left a prayer request. I doubt that I slept at all. I called my Dad in Lubbock at 6:30 a.m. because I knew it was Dad's practice to pray in the morning with his men's group. I put in another call to Arizona to speak to Chris and Michael—Howard's grown children—to let them know their Dad was in the hospital. I then called the rest of my family. I could not sleep. When I got back to the hospital, they had not done the biopsy yet. I tried to encourage Howard and we prayed. I read one of my favorite verses out of the Bible: "For I know the thoughts that I think toward you, saith the LORD, thoughts of peace, and not of evil, to give you an expected end. Then shall ye call upon me, and ye shall go and pray unto me, and I will hearken unto you. And ye shall seek me, and find me, when ye shall search for me with all your heart."

"And ye shall seek me, and find me..."

Jeremiah 29:11-13

Then, they came for Howard. It was time for the biopsy...

– From Beverley's Journal

I think your house transcends into a temple of peace after you've been spending time in a hospital bed and eating hospital food.

Tranquility was short-lived. Two days after I was home from the first biopsy, they called and informed me that the sample, a piece of liver tissue, was inconclusive. A second biopsy was necessary, this time to be performed under ultrasound.

"Tranquility was short-lived."

Back in the hospital, another biopsy attempt, and another trip home, to be greeted enthusiastically by Daisy. Anyone watching how she greeted me with growls deep in her chest and bared teeth (she was actually smiling) would think we were mortal enemies, instead of the best of buddies.

Waiting for biopsy reports is an activity that will do wonders for your prayer life. Waiting and praying. And growing anxious, I have to admit. One good remedy for anxiety is to focus your concern on someone else, which is just what we did.

A Fellow Traveler Beckons

"We had never gotten together outside church."

Rick was a church friend who was struggling with a devastating esophageal cancer. He was having a terrible time, yet he had enough concern for *my* outcome to write me. We never had gotten together outside church, so his email insisted I "stop messing around" and pay him a visit.

When I got his email, I was recuperating from the two biopsies and awaiting the final verdict—hopefully—from the second test, so I had time on my hands. We decided to pay Rick a visit.

Rick lived outside Fort Worth in a rural area. Bev and I did not ask if they could use some help—we simply stopped at

Kentucky Fried Chicken and loaded up with boxes of chicken and fixin's and soft drinks and brought them a fast-food feast. Rick's family seemed appreciative and, God bless them, they clearly were very hungry.

Stress has that effect and the body still has to be fed, regardless of the current emotional situation. But Rick could not eat.

"...the body still has to be fed..."

We found Rick propped up in bed with his ever-present laptop computer in front of him as he peered through swollen eyes and over bloated cheeks at the real estate ventures and land development plans he had on his computer screen.

Rick's face was edematous (swollen from fluid accumulation) from the treatments he had received and it must have been painful, but I never saw him downtrodden. Never.

As I leaned close to him, he was forced to whisper his communications to me, telling me that he hoped to make more progress in his land development, in order to benefit his wife should he not survive the cancer. He whispered this to me while he glanced at his wife across the room where she stood talking to Bev. As if his wife did not suspect he might be departing the earthly realm. An amazing man. Grace and courage and a gentle spirit. What a great example for a guy like me...a guy waiting for his own biopsy report.

"Grace and courage and a gentle spirit."

So, we visited and talked and laughed. I even performed an impromptu rap song—don't ask me why—which brought some needed comical relief into their home. We did our best to encourage Rick and his family, and then we headed home, back to our own worries and doubts.

On the drive back to Fort Worth, I wondered: what were *my* odds…my odds of beating this? From a medical perspective, a real toss-up, I supposed. From God's perspective, there were no "odds," just His decision. I asked Him what was coming, but He wasn't saying at the moment.

If I had cancer, then I needed to maintain the fight—like Rick did—while still trying to live my life with meaning. If it turned out to be a benign cyst—the veritable Golden Fleece—then I could (and should) re-devote myself to live above mediocrity—to meet the daily drudgery with a brand new attitude and a new purpose.

This lofty ideal sounded to me like a "New Life" resolution (instead of a New Year's). If given a chance, I would do this or that. Have a better attitude, be a better person. You know. But you and I also know how people are about keeping such resolutions.

A Time For Thanksgiving

That time of waiting was also a time for giving thanks. Thanksgiving Day was approaching and I had a sneaking hunch that I would be asked to say grace over the Thanksgiving meal with Bev's family.

"Jesus, please teach me to appreciate what I have, before time forces me to appreciate what I had."

The *Fort Worth Star-Telegram* was running a series on peoples' favorite Thanksgiving prayers. I dug through the several pages of this special article and found just the thing: a simple, but fitting prayer, short and sweet.

It said, *"Jesus, please teach me to appreciate what I have, before time forces me to appreciate what I had."* The prayer was credited to a Susan L. Lenzkes. Fitting and appropriate, I thought.

I cast a glance over the newspaper at my wife as she prepared dinner. And here, I thought, was truly something—some*one*—for whom to be grateful. My wife, companion, and soon-to-be caregiver.

Lessons Learned

1. The caregiver, especially if a family member, quickly assumes the roles of information officer, home manager, and emotional cheerleader. The bills still have to be paid, the dog fed, etc. Clearly, this role can become overwhelming without some external support.
2. Develop a thankful heart for your blessings, no matter how small they seem to be.
3. Help others when you can. It takes your mind off your own troubles.
4. Take your fears and anxiety to God. He can handle them.

Chapter 3: *Diagnosis*

A week later, Howard was at work in a medical clinic when his physician (who is also Howard's supervisor) called Howard into the office. In the hand of the physician was a pathology report. The biopsy result was finally in.

The doctor asked Howard to sit down and then the doctor laid the results on the desk. I remember Howard telling me that when he read the report, he felt as though the air physically had been knocked out of him.

"The biopsy result was finally in."

The doctor called me at home to give me the results: "B-cell Lymphoma." I had no idea what that was, but I was to learn over the next year. But Lymphoma had an ugly sound.

The doctor told me that he had patients that had this particular type of cancer for 15 years and that they were still doing fine. He also told me that he was scheduling Howard to see an Oncologist for further assessment and that it was vitally important that, from that moment on, I should attend every oncology appointment Howard would have.

"This was a family disease, the doctor explained..."

This was a family disease, the doctor explained, and spouse and family support would be vital to a good outcome. Plus, I could ask questions that were of concern and possibly bring up issues that Howard, under treatment and stress, might forget.

Amazingly, so the physician went on to tell me, Howard—just after learning this news—went right back to work seeing his own patients.

Before we disconnected, the doctor also told me that next would come what they call "staging," a method of determining the extent of the cancer. Staging would help them decide the prognosis and the treatment.

Howard would be scheduled for a bone marrow biopsy, a colonoscopy, and a battery of blood tests. Finally, he would have a PET scan—a special type of X-ray that shows cancer activity by its amount of glucose uptake. We would also be seeing a surgeon for removal of Howard's gallbladder.

We continued to seek God's wisdom for the physicians and for ourselves.

Feeling it was critical to make informed decisions, Howard started utilizing the Internet to research the treatment and surgeries indicated for lymphoma.
– From Beverley's Journal

My boss sat me down in his office and placed a report in front of me. My gaze, by habit, skimmed down to where it said *"Impression: Large B-cell non-Hodgkin's lymphoma."* It was a shock to see it in black and white. Just like that: I was a cancer patient.

"Just like that: I was a cancer patient."

He watched me carefully, ready to reassure me. And what could I do, cry? Whine? His own daughter was, at that time, doing poorly with recurring breast cancer and metastases. The doc and I both knew his daughter's time on this earth was dwindling. But nevertheless, this was me we were talking about.

"You okay?" He asked.

I glanced up and nodded. "Yeah, I'm great."

37

"Listen, Howard. I've got some patients going on 15 years with this diagnosis, and they're doing fine. It's not a bad cancer to have if you have to have one."

The room was still feeling wobbly and anxiety gnawed at my gut, but I nodded. "Would you mind telling my wife that on the phone? She'll need some encouragement." It seemed that, of late, doctors were giving my wife all kinds of bad tidings, but I thought hearing from him would be reassuring to her.

"Would you mind telling my wife that?"

As he made the call, I read the report again, but the words stayed the same. Despite being a pretty good family practice PA and an assistant professor with the local medical university, I was not an expert on lymphoma and I did not often meet cancer patients. I would have some reading to do.

Five minutes later, I headed back down the long corridor of the clinic to see my own patients. And my schedule was pretty stacked up by then. People with colds and coughs, others needing refills of medications to manage diabetes and hypertension. I doubted any of them were facing chemotherapy. Nevertheless, to every patient, their own problems were tantamount.

"It would be one day at a time."

Honestly, I don't know where I found the gumption to continue with clinic that afternoon, as if nothing had happened. Maybe I was in a small state of shock, or in denial, or maybe I just realized that—from then on—it would be one day at a time. My life had changed, no going back, only forward…wherever that happened to lead.

Lessons Learned

1. Take one day at a time.

2. Research recommended surgeries and treatments.
3. Make decisions that you feel are best for you.
4. Look to God for peace and strength, regardless of the outcome.

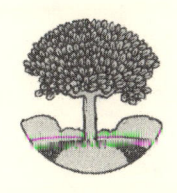

Chapter 4: *Journey Preparations*

It was vitally important for us that Howard get in touch with Human Resources right away and sign up for the FMLA (Family Medical Leave Act). With that protection, we would not have to worry about Howard losing his job when he got sick or was hospitalized.

"...sign up for the FMLA..."

Appointments were being scheduled almost every day. I bought a little planner/calendar that I kept in my purse, and every appointment and instruction that I received went right into this and then was transferred to my main calendar at home. I collected business cards from the physicians and nurses at the Cancer Center and I brought *back with me cards from our pharmacy and gave them to each provider involved in Howard's care, in case they needed to call in prescriptions. I kept all important phone numbers by the phone.*

We had our first appointment with the Oncologist who told us how he would like to treat this. He wanted us to go to the M.D. Anderson Medical Center in Houston for another biopsy and to have the treatments there, but Howard declined and said he wanted to stay in town. Also, an additional surgery that the oncologist proposed—to surgically remove part of Howard's liver—was turned down by Howard who, after doing research, felt that the risk was too high.

"...an additional surgery..."

To complicate things, Daisy, our sweet dog of 13 years, had diabetes and needed two shots a day of insulin. Giving these shots was something I had to learn to do—something very traumatic for both Daisy and me.

Howard and I had an orientation meeting in the chemo room of the Cancer Center with a nurse. She showed us a video, went over a list of things to expect, and then opened the floor for questions.

I learned that there were certain foods and vitamins that should not be taken during actual days of treatment. Some things we learned in the briefing, but a lot we would learn as we experienced it. All of the nurses were compassionate and very patient with us.

Tests proceeded and another concern arose: a hot spot in the colon appeared on the PET scan.

We saw the surgeon the end of January and he booked the Operating Room for Feb. 5th 2007. The surgeon planned to *remove Howard's gallbladder, appendix and a portion of his colon, due to a spot that had shown up on the PET scan.*

"...he had Howard on his prayer list."

The surgeon was a wonderful compassionate Christian man who we really trusted and liked. He told us he had Howard on his prayer list. You don't hear that very often.

– From Beverley's Journal

The oncology center, officially known as "The Center for Cancer and Blood Disorders," was on Montgomery Street, a quaint area of Fort Worth decorated with old Victorian buildings and somewhat eccentric cafés. But the Center itself was modern and very efficient. Inside, I found veteran cancer patients, most of them female, pale, tired-looking, and wearing hats or scarves on their heads. Their facial features also were pretty much devoid of hair. Soon, I realized, I would look like them, blend in, and become part of the family.

"Soon...I would look like them, blend in, and become part of the family."

The Oncologist

The oncologist was very distinguished looking and very reputable. I would describe him as professional, competent, and very busy. He was high on the list of senior physicians and he chronically ran late...*way* late on his appointments with us. At first, it was okay, but it wore on

45

me—any unnecessary waiting—as my strength eventually lapsed. But the things I needed at that moment were access to the system, clear-thinking medical decision-making, and not necessarily touchy-feely sentiment.

Despite the second biopsy being positive, the oncologist suggested I have a liver resection to get another, more confirmatory, specimen.

Later, at home, an Internet search gave me the necessary information to make an informed decision about the resection.

"...the necessary information to make an informed decision..."

With one biopsy in the bag, I did not want to take the risk with this particular surgery. I told this to the surgeon on the telephone. The surgeon agreed with me. The liver resection was too dangerous.

After our initial appointment with the oncologist Bev and I toured the facility.

The cancer center had its own laboratory and radiology facilities, a chemotherapy treatment wing, and was one of the few centers with a "cyber knife," a very precise, less invasive way of employing radiation therapies to treat hard to get-to anatomical locations. We headed upstairs to meet the nurses who ran the chemotherapy treatment area.

The Chemo Floor

The chemo area took up the entire wing upstairs. We entered an open bay clustered with rows of green leather reclining chairs where patients received their treatments. Over the patients, like a bright school of jellyfish, were suspended multi-colored bags of IV fluids from which IV lines descended like tentacles.

The nurses were extremely friendly, but also extremely busy, flitting from patient to patient and adjusting IV drips.

Bev and I were shown to a private room, in order to review and sign the informed consents, one for each chemotherapeutic agent I would receive.

Undergoing chemotherapy would be quite an experience, I knew, but signing the consent forms for the chemo drugs was an eye-opener as well.

"Signing the consent forms for the chemo drugs was an eye-opener..."

Some pretty big guns were coming my way. Very aggressive treatment, a combination known to oncologists as CHOP-R. Cytoxan, Vincristine, Adriamycin, and a "monoclonal antibody" called Rituximab fashioned from mouse cells.

Oh, yes, and lots of steroids in the oral form of Prednisone. But first, Bev and I had to review the consent forms and sign that we understood the risks.

After I reviewed the potential complications of the chemotherapy—everything from peripheral neuropathy to heart valve damage—I asked the nurse whether anyone had ever refused to sign these things.

The nurse answered, "There was just such a man yesterday."

"You mean, he didn't sign?" I asked.

She nodded, more interested in getting *me* to sign than to tell me stories. But she went on. "He read through his drug forms and than he up and left." She shrugged. "He'll be back. The treatment is tough, but it's life-saving for many."

So, the treatment plan was drawn up and read and signed. But the chemo would have to wait until I recuperated from the pending surgeries. There would be about an eight week delay, to allow the wounds to close up. Chemotherapy would have disrupted the healing process.

There was a lot on my plate, but my heart went out to Bev, who sat beside me and listened, asked questions, and took notes.

Views On A Caregiver

Having cancer is bad, but the caregiver's story must be pretty tough. The pain the caregiver feels is the emotional kind and there would be physical labor involved in caring for someone who is ill. Add to that the concerns about medical insurance, mortgage payments, feeding the cancer patient, and, in this case, feeding our dog and giving her insulin injections—a chore that I previously attended to, but might not be able to handle at times, now. All this could overwhelm anyone.

"The pain the caregiver feels is the emotional kind..."

The caregiver also has to contend with driving, scheduling and tracking appointments, getting the oral medications and the home-administered injections ready (when applicable) for the patient. Then there would be preparing meals, cleaning up after the patient, and, no doubt, sometimes being scared to death but careful not to show it.

"If you could describe such a caregiver in one word, it would be 'give.'"

And if the cancer patient is truly blessed with a wonderful spouse doubling as caregiver, your spouse/caregiver may even be willing to have a romantic session with you despite your very unromantic appearance.

If you could describe such a caregiver in one word, it would be "give." But actually, you should multiply that, because, in time, it becomes "give, give, give, and give."

Advice For Caregiver And Patient

Some practical advice for caregivers: attend every appointment with the patient. Ask questions and make notes of the answers. The patient will be overwhelmed or ill and may not remember to ask the right questions or he may be dealing with "chemo brain." Sexual relations should not be within three or four days of chemotherapy. I'm not sure about the status of pregnant caregivers, or for that matter pregnant patients receiving chemotherapy or being indirectly exposed to chemo. Ask your oncologist.

"FMLA, the Family Medical Leave Act, can be a job-saving measure."

For the patient: FMLA, the Family Medical Leave Act, can be a job-saving measure. Be sure to complete an application, if it applies in your situation, as soon as possible including your medical condition, expected doctor visits, and other potential absences. This requires you to document sick leave and to submit it periodically to your employer's human resources office.

A New Wrinkle

As the tests continued, a PET scan revealed what you might call "hotspots," in the glands of my neck, in my liver, and in a vague area of my terminal ileum (part of the lower colon). The neck region was decided to be benign, just inflammation, but the area in the colon was definitely suspicious-appearing.

The original surgery plan expanded. Now, it became plans to remove the gallbladder (with its gallstone lodged in a duct), the appendix, and the portion of my colon that lit up on the PET scan.

Before the surgery, I had one last biopsy—just to be sure—this one of my bone marrow. It was relatively painless.

Daisy And Me

At about this time, our yellow Labrador Retriever, Daisy, was having her own problems with chemo and treatments.

It was found that she had Cushing's disease, a rare condition in humans, but a lot more common in dogs. She had a reaction to chemo-like medication intended to treat the Cushing's and then she needed prednisone to treat the initial reaction…and the prednisone played havoc with her diabetes control. She lost weight steadily and experienced bouts of weakness.

"It was a ritual we went through every day when I came home…"

She was a sweet dog. She would welcome me home from work with her hind end up in the air and her front paws stretched out while she growled at me as if I were a burglar. It was a ritual we went through every day when I came home from work, but I took note that lately that ritual was becoming less and less frequent.

There was a time later—when chemotherapy started slamming me pretty hard—that Daisy weakly made her way over to where I rested on the couch. We were a pair, she and I. She was fast losing weight and I was losing all my hair. She looked up at me with soulful almond-shaped eyes as I gently cupped her frail jaw in my hand and wondered which one of us was going to go first.

Lessons Learned
1. Stay in prayer.
2. Caregivers should attend all appointments possible, gather information, and take notes. Get a planner—there will be many appointments to track.
3. Sign up for FMLA through your Human Resources Department.
4. Seek God's wisdom in your and your doctor's

decisions.
5. Ask questions. When uncertain, ask again.

Chapter 5: *Surgery and the Soul*

The night before the surgery, God answered my prayers and granted my husband a peaceful sleep.

The weather was so cold the next morning. The Senior and Associate Pastors of our church were there just before Howard was taken into surgery. They prayed with us and joked with Howard, who has a really good sense of humor and showed it even then.

About four hours later, Howard was brought back to his room. His voice was hoarse and he was complaining of pain from a large abdominal incision through which the surgeon had explored Howard's intestine. Howard has a pretty high threshold for pain, but they had a morphine pump connected to his IV.

The surgeon stopped by and told me that when he went in to remove part of Howard's colon, the operating team could find nothing—no cancerous area—that warranted removing part of the colon. During the operation, the surgeon had brought in two other doctors, but the three of them could not locate a lymphoma mass, so they called the oncologist, who, in turn, had a radiologist look at the previous films (all this in the OR while the colon was still exposed) and finally, the surgeon determined that they would put Howard's colon back into the abdomen without resecting it. (Thank you Lord.)

> "The three of them could not locate a lymphoma mass..."

Howard had a rough time in the hospital and hallucinated from the morphine. He completely lost track of what time it was. One night, he called me from the hospital and asked me to call the surgeon at home and get him to release Howard from the hospital. I told Howard we would have to wait; it was almost 10:00 at night. Howard was certain that it was 10:00 a.m., not 10:00 p.m.

At home, Howard's recovery was long and painful. He had many sleepless nights trying to find a position that was comfortable because of the large incision. One night his pain was so bad I had to call the surgeon who had kindly given me his cell phone number.

It was the middle of the night and he returned my call within 15 minutes. I could tell I had awakened him, but he listened

"He was such a blessing from God to us."

attentively to what I said and gave me instructions and further, he wanted me to call his office the next morning to let him know how Howard was doing. How many surgeons do you know that would give you their cell phone number? He was such a blessing from God to us.

Howard was plagued with problems from that abdominal incision as it widened beyond its original borders and refused to heal. I got him a little pillow that he tucked into his waistband; we kept him in comfortable jogging suits. Soon, we would begin chemotherapy treatments (notice, I said "we"), but first Howard had to have a port-a-cath put into his chest to receive the IV chemotherapy meds; the drugs they would be giving in chemo would be too rough on his veins. Fortunately, the port-a-cath surgery was a day surgery and Howard was able to return home the same day.

"It was becoming obvious that we weren't getting the support..."

Our pastor came to visit and there were some "get well" cards and phone calls. But it was becoming obvious that we weren't getting the support from our Sunday School class or other church friends that we might have expected. (One elderly couple from the seniors group at church came to visit several times, both in the hospital and at our home.) It seemed so strange that the people that we thought were our good friends from church—after we had been members there for seven years—never came to visit and very few called. Even the phone calls tapered off. It became a very quiet time, indeed.

Howard said I made excuses for them. I knew how some people had trouble dealing with surgeries and illnesses. Another cancer patient I met at the Center told me how some people wouldn't touch her or get near to her, as if cancer were contagious.

"...some people wouldn't touch her..."

God's hand was in all of this—this strange isolation—and I believe He had something He wanted us to learn: to look up to Him and not to focus on other people. If we had had a lot of support from our church, we would have looked to them for encouragement, strength, and dependence. Instead, it was a daily walk with God. A silent walk, but

God, even in His silence, was revealing himself to Howard and me in a way that we would have otherwise never experienced.

I watched Howard pour through his Bible every morning and read Streams in the Desert, a wonderful devotional book compiled by a missionary's wife. Honestly, though, I will have to say that, in my flesh, I would get to feeling rejected and abandoned by our church family. But our faith and our relationship with the Lord grew more than I can express. "...That your faith should not stand in the wisdom of man, but in the power of God." 1 Corinthians 2:4-5.

We would sit on the couch and watch several sermons on television each week, Howard being in too much pain to consider church. One program in particular really spoke to us. It was a sermon in November 2006, just after Howard's diagnosis.

The preacher asked the question: why does God allow us to suffer? Sometimes, the preacher went on to say, it is to get our attention.

As we went through those terrible trials with cancer, God taught us empathy for others going through similar circumstances. "..that we may be able to comfort them which are in any trouble, by the comfort wherewith we ourselves are comforted." 2 Corinthians 1:3-4.

– From Beverley's Journal

They took out my gallbladder and appendix, but could find no cancerous masses in the colon. The consensus was to close me back up without removing the terminal ileum portion of my colon.

I had a real problem with that lower abdominal incision and I had to think it was due to them yanking and squeezing on my intestine. It seemed to give me an inordinate amount of pain.

Post-op Delusions

During my post-op time in the hospital, I partook of a morphine drip for the first and only time in my life, and I had some very interesting delusions and hallucinations. I still remember them distinctly.

One time, I called my wife complaining that it was 10 a.m. and that she had not shown up to visit me. She patiently explained over the phone that it was actually 10 p.m. and past visiting hours.

I was further gone than that; I was convinced a cult had taken over the hospital floor. I told her, "You need to get me out of here! They get together at night when everyone else is gone. I can hear their leader giving them orders to visit each patient." What exactly I thought they were going to do to the patients, I don't remember, but I was convinced of my conspiracy theory, fed by the morphine drip.

How real that delusion still seems.

It didn't help matters that later, the incision would have to be reopened.

"That's what surgeons do," I told Bev en route to the surgical follow-up appointment. "Just watch." The incision site seemed infected; it hurt like a boil and it was mean-looking, swollen, and purple. I also knew darn well that the surgeon's first inclination would be to reopen the surgical site…which is exactly what he did—right there in the exam room on our follow-up appointment. No hesitation (and no local anesthesia, mind you.) There was not much skin sensation, superficially, but boy—it hurt to walk around and I got used to keeping a small pillow stuffed between my waist band and my abdomen.

"My workplace started getting a little impatient..."

I was having a long recovery in the hospital and at home. My workplace starting getting a little impatient, wanting to know when I would come back. Two months was the agreement for my surgical recuperation period, but that was before the reopening of the incision site. And yes, they knew I would be facing chemotherapy as well.

But to be fair, my job was to see patients. And patients require appointments, and to make appointments, you have to know when the doc (or in my case, the PA) will be in the clinic to see them.

I had a final surgery, though, the placement of a port a cath—a small disc about the diameter of a half-dollar piece. They inserted it under the skin of my upper left chest wall; this provided a convenient access where the nurses would be inserting a catheter to administer the chemo agents.

The port-a-cath placement was done during a day surgery and didn't cause me pain; it has not caused me problems to this day, though I have a natural dislike for having a foreign object in my chest (other patients I'd spoken to felt the same way). Nevertheless, I was glad to have it—and to spare my veins from those every-three-week chemo sessions. The drugs they would be giving me would have ruined my veins in no time.

It was a long haul, getting over that abdominal surgery wound. Lots of time to get into scripture and to contemplate this whole cancer business.

Affliction

Facing cancer brings God to one's mind. Let's face it: it's about facing your mortality…and your Maker. That old saw about adversity making you either "bitter or better" also seems to apply here. Our pastor said that God had entrusted me with cancer, but I had no desire to inspire anyone with how I faced this "journey." When I was ill or really hurting, I did not see cancer as a "gift" or a test, but just a misery, a potential sidetrack to my life's intended destination, an unfair punishment from a vengeful, unseen Maker. I didn't spend my time crying or whining, but sometimes I certainly felt sorry for myself.

"I did not see cancer as a 'gift…'"

Then, one evening, I saw my Bible lying there on the table. And beside the Bible, a daily devotional with pretty nifty stories that I remembered were inspiring. I started reading.

Scriptures about affliction seemed especially pertinent. Prayers and psalms about suffering and asking for mercy. It seemed the Biblical David and I both felt afflicted, but neither of us wanted to die, and both of us were quite willing to humble ourselves and ask for favor. I have that much, at least, in common with a king.

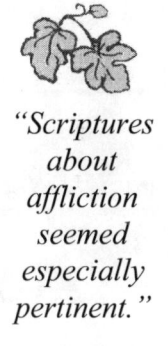

"Scriptures about affliction seemed especially pertinent."

But for some reason, another striking passage stood out, this one from Isaiah, only it was not so much about affliction. It was about trusting too much in yourself. It seemed an odd time to discover this passage.

It warned against those who would build their own fire and "encompass themselves amidst their own sparks" instead of following God's direction. In this scripture, the response from the Lord—His promise—was that those following their own way would, when they lie down, they would lie down in sorrow.

"Who is among you that feareth the LORD, that obeyeth the voice of his servant, that walketh in darkness, and hath no light? Let him trust in the name of the LORD, and stay upon his God. Behold, all ye that kindle a fire, that compass yourselves about with sparks: walk in the light of your fire, and in the sparks that ye have kindled. This shall ye have of mine hand; ye shall lie down in sorrow." Isaiah 50:10-11

I was doing a fair amount of lying down in sorrow lately.

I took it as a warning about creating my own light, following my own way without consulting God. Too many leaders, pastors, and common folk like me create their own light, their own "vision," their own plans, rather than waiting upon the Lord. Being a person of impulse with the bad habit of making impetuous decisions, I believe this scripture was directed at me. I include this concern here because it was part of my cancer process and part of the peculiar timing of God we sometimes encounter. If you are a deliberate person and one who habitually seeks wisdom from above before making decisions, and you don't depend too much upon the charity of others (even in the midst of personal storms), then you are a wiser person than I.

"This proved to be a time of isolation."

At a time when it would be good to have support from all sides, this proved to be a time of isolation. Maybe that's why the previous scripture caught my eye.

Church Politics

I had been a trustee in a large local church and a member of a 50-plus member Sunday School class. It was unfortunate timing, it seemed to me, to discover some ministry decisions that, as a trustee and a church member, I could not agree with. I tendered my resignation as a trustee, but maintained my church membership…and, I thought, maintained my church friendships. But I might as well have cancelled my membership while I was at it.

We received cards and well wishes from church members, but not one visit from our Sunday School class during the cancer treatments which lasted April to August. It was a strange silence. A strange abandonment. *Truly, thou art a God who hides Himself,* I thought. But I was missing the point. God speaks to us, but sometimes we just don't understand the language.

"Truly, thou art a God who hides Himself."

One day, my wife took a telephone call from a Sunday School member, a woman of high standing in the class and church community. The woman was calling to ask my wife to come help decorate the Sunday School classroom for Christmas. My wife, hurt and amazed, told the woman that it was not a good time, considering my struggle with cancer and all that it demanded of my wife's energy. "Oh," the woman said, "How's he doing?" It was a short conversation.

Dark Night of the Soul

"A painful time, but a time of growth..."

One evening, I read an article about the "*dark night of the soul*" and how this dark time affected Mother Teresa, of all people. It described how her diaries revealed times of spiritual isolation when she cried out for God but could not sense His presence. Her faith weakened. Doubts crept in. But still, she persevered, she prayed, she ministered, and she worshipped in silence, never abandoning her faith, though *she* felt abandoned.

Mother Teresa's isolation was likened to "the dark night of the soul," a situation described by an ancient holy man named Saint John of the Cross (not the Apostle John). The dark night of the soul, as this later John described, was a time of isolation from human support, from human spiritual ministering, when you walked alone with the Lord and leaned only upon Him, or more accurately, leaned upon what you knew He expected of you.

A painful time, but a time of growth and increased personal relationship with God. A level of relationship some people do not experience. Maybe all cancer patients, if turned toward things of God, share this narrow, lonely road with the saints and the prophets. Maybe we cancer patients all experience it at some point, no matter how many friends or family members or church people we have coming to our aid. Maybe there *is* purpose in suffering.

But if it were not for Bev's family, we would have had to hire help. I'm not sure that the lack of support is pleasing to God, but He makes use of it. Some people still think if you are afflicted, there must be sin in your life. Tell that to the parents of a six-year-old child with terminal cancer. Tell that to innocent victims of hit-and-run drunk drivers. God uses affliction to get our attention, but sometimes—as a popular televangelist, David Jeremiah, (who himself dealt with cancer) said—cancer mostly comes our way because our world is broken and diseased.

"Our world is broken and diseased."

Bev and I were sitting in a little Chinese restaurant where I could count on great hot-and-sour soup and a quiet meal when we ran into a friend from church. He told us that a girl with breast cancer—a young mother of two and a long-time church member—lost her home because the family struggled to pay their bills. Their plight was long-known to the church. Finally, the mother had died. The financial burden of this family was obvious (we did help financially, but it was not enough and not in time.)

So, why did the loss of their home happen? My friend

thought it was because the mother and her husband did not ask for help. "Out of pride," he said. Pride? Or was the church that oblivious to that family's need?

Christians can let you down—just like any people. Everyone has his own troubles, his own struggles, his own weaknesses. Christians, and all human beings, will let you down. But, their behavior does not change who God is.

So how does this all relate? Bible passages from prophets and revelations from mystics?

Because, for cancer patients and their loved ones, this is a time in your lives when you have to step carefully, one step at a time with limited vision, but with unlimited faith.

It makes me think of the Jewish prayer closet. I see images of Jesus isolating Himself. In a sense he's creating a prayer closet and leaving the world for a moment to concentrate on the voice of God. He did that in Gethsemane and He did that in the mountains and barren wastes.

Sometimes God speaks with a small still voice, a voice that you cannot hear if you're talking constantly...or even if you're constantly praying. Sometimes *listening* is the key...and walking by God's light rather than creating your own.

Lessons Learned.
1. People will let you down. It does not change who God is. He will never let you down.
2. It is our responsibility to discern when people are suffering. Do not assume someone else is helping. Ease the burdens of others.
3. Feel confident in your attending physicians and surgeons. If you lack confidence, discuss it with them or seek second opinions.
4. Talk to God, be frank with Him, and ask what He wants you to learn.

Chapter 6: *Chemo*

Howard's first treatment was on April 4th, 2007. The nurses on the chemo floor were very warm people. They did everything they could to make patients comfortable.

That morning, we made our first mistake—a big one. Howard was supposed to have taken 100 mg of Prednisone prior to arrival at the Cancer Center, in order to keep him from having a reaction to the chemo drugs, but through some misfire, we had not received the prescription in time. Howard would pay the price later that day.

On future visits, we discovered that if he took 5 tablets (10 mg. each, for a total of 50 mg.) on the morning of the chemo treatment and then the other 5 tablets when he got home, he could tolerate the Prednisone (it tended to tear up his stomach) and he still would have it in his system when he most needed it to counteract the adverse chemo effects. The nurses also gave him something for nausea in the IV during what they called pre-treatment, the initial IV bag that also contained Benadryl to fight potential allergic reactions.

I had prepared a little food carrier—a type of insulated lunchbox—and filled it with light snacks. The carrier would keep food cool and fresh. I had been warned to keep snacks light, in order to prevent nausea.

"I had been warned to keep snacks light..."

Every chemo treatment would take a full eight hours, due to the number of drugs they would run through the IV. I left him there in the green chair and would come back to pick him up at the end of the day. He agreed to call me when it was about a half hour from the completion of treatment, giving me enough time to come for him, but not keeping him waiting. I would have stayed the entire day, but he insisted I go and, frankly, the chemo floor is not designed to cater to families.

I would call the nurses mid-day to check on him. All during the day and on the way home, I prayed for him.

I was grateful to see him perky and smiling when I returned. From his green recliner, he looked up at me and said, "This was a piece of cake. And speaking of cake, I'm hungry. Let's go get some Mexican Food on the way home."

The nurse looked very dubious. She said she would not recommend a heavy meal unless Howard wanted to "revisit" that food again.

She administered an injection of Neulasta, a drug to help keep Howard's white count from plummeting, and then we *were officially done with the first chemotherapy session. It did seem surprisingly easy on Howard, after all.*

We had not reached the car before Howard felt a slight chill. He did not think much of it, but we should have turned back. On the way home, Howard started shivering and shaking violently. At his insistence, I stopped at a McDonald's to get him a hot cup of coffee, but most of it spilled on the car floor; he was shaking too hard to drink it.

By the time we got home, he had a fever of 103 and started vomiting. Just as I got the oncologist on the phone, Howard's fever dropped to 101 and he started feeling better.

This was Day One of his chemotherapy. He would have a total of eight treatments, each treatment three weeks apart.

– From Beverley's Journal

"What are you in for?" The elderly patient in the battered Cowboys cap asked me.

Privacy was not available (or even desirable, I soon would find out) in this place. But what was there to be ashamed or bashful about? Nothing. "Lymphoma," I said.

"Oh, yeah?" He grinned at me. "Me, too. This is my second time. Got treated the first time eight years ago."

Great. That was not encouraging to hear.

Beside him, another patient, a thin middle-aged woman, was staring at me. I asked her if she were okay.

"No!" She yelled, and she began to gasp and grow quite pale. She was having a reaction to the chemo. I hollered for help and the nurses swarmed in to tend to the woman.

As some attended to the agitated woman, other nurses helped those of us in the immediate area to find new chairs in a different section. (So much for my prime spot.) Suddenly, I was no longer concerned about privacy; we all had to be visible to the nurses. Supervision was constant.

After the brief hullabaloo, I settled down and a nurse got me started on my actual chemo meds. So far, no adverse reactions.

"...a type of grace in her suffering..."

I saw another female patient wheeled-in on a gurney by a couple ambulance attendants. The woman's scalp was swathed in a cloth hat, resembling a type of headdress and she looked regal in a way, as if she were a royal personage being transported on an ancient palanquin. But while she had a type of grace in her suffering, she also looked near death and in agony. Her skin was gray and her facial features were stretched tight in discomfort.

I felt compassion and admiration for this woman. I also felt a swell of empathy for all the cancer patients on the floor. We were a sad lot, but folks were chatting, reading magazines, others sleeping. We were plugging along, surviving, living as best we could under the circumstances. A moan turned my attention back to the new arrival.

She was misery and dignity co-inhabiting a failing body. She was groaning in pain and obviously quite nauseated. They wheeled her into a private room, where I assume she received chemo.

"Don't eat any of your favorite foods during chemo..."

Things were quiet for a while.

The Chemo Routine

I snacked occasionally on cheese sticks and crackers (even now, the thought of cheese sticks brings up a ball of nausea in my stomach). A warning: don't eat any of your favorite foods during chemo, because you may well develop an aversion to them even beyond your treatment time. Certain foods thereafter become associated with chemo. For me, it was cheese sticks, cheese pizza, and small chocolate chip cookies. (Even typing that last sentence is making me a little queasy. Funny how the mind works.)

A wannabe novelist, I intended to keep a journal of the cancer experience and to integrate it into a book idea I had. I contemplated giving the hero of my story cancer, but ultimately, I thought it would be better to let folks read what *I* experienced, rather than through some fictional character. That required some real soul-searching on my part.

But I didn't get much consistent writing done. As the chemo treatments progressed, it was all I could do to drag myself onto a green chair and take in another eight hours of toxic substances designed to keep me alive even as it felt like they were pushing me toward oblivion. And the nausea meds I needed in larger increments pretty much wiped me out. To be honest, I slept through the bulk of treatments.

But everyone, at some point, has to get up and wheel their portable IV pole to the restroom. And grab a cup of coffee. That was one thing that never became an aversion and it warmed me up and even helped with the nausea. Coffee was my friend.

Hours later, they wheeled the woman on the gurney from her room. She still looked ill and gray, but she looked toward the nurse's station and managed to whisper the words, "Thank you" as she was transported toward the exit. No one but I saw her mouth those words—no one but God and I. It was an amazing display of courage and dignity.

"...an amazing display of courage and dignity."

Compared to these poor folks, my chemo seemed like a piece of cake. But one word of advice to patients getting treatment on the busy oncology floor: *don't be afraid to speak up.* As they hung my last IV bag, I noticed they did not plug it into the automated IV machine, the machine on a pole that counts out the drops in prescribed timing. They forgot to plug it in. I nodded off—and no one noticed that the last IV bag was not connected. That kept me there an hour longer than necessary.

Treatment One Completed

My first chemo was done, but the steroids would go on another five days. Another chemo patient had warned me about the possible effects of steroids (the oral form I took was Prednisone.) Although the huge amounts of Prednisone I would end up taking did not lead me to the bouts of psychosis I was warned against, I probably seemed a little off my rocker.

One time, in the midst of the heavy Prednisone course, I woke my wife at three in the morning with what I just knew was a remarkable discovery in my Bible reading. Ha ha.

Bev, awakened from a deep sleep, stared at me for a moment, then said, "That's very interesting, but maybe you should get in bed, honey. You're supposed to be working this morning."

But, back to the first chemo treatment…

First Treatment, First Reaction

I admit to feeling a little cocky. Things seemed to go more easily than I expected. I was even hungry. "This was a piece of cake," I remember telling my wife when she picked me up. Foolish mortal.

I did not make it to the car before I was shaking and feverish. The shakes became tremors and then full-fledged rigors wracking my torso until I thought my ribs would break. We were half-way home by then and no turning back; the cancer center would be closed. We made it home and Bev was dialing the doc while I fought the urge to bring up those cheese sticks. My temperature was 103.

"I was wimping out already."

Funny, but what ultimately helped was the dreaded vomiting I fought so hard to avoid. When it came up, my temp immediately dropped by two degrees and the shakes subsided. Obviously, not an infection so soon. I was having a reaction to the chemo agents.

"Is it going to be like this every time, doc?" I asked the oncologist on the telephone. "If it is, I don't think I'm going to be able to handle it." I was wimping out already.

"We'll give you additional medication the next time. Didn't you take your prednisone?"

I had not, not knowing it was supposed to precede the chemotherapy. I remedied the situation, added Advil and Gatorade at Bev's insistence, and soon things calmed down.

My co-workers, knowing I had my first treatment, greeted me with amazement the next morning. But I was symptom-free that day. My employers kindly provided me a surgical mask and sterile gloves to wear whenever I was examining potentially contagious patients.

Lessons Learned

1. Make sure the proper prescriptions are filled and taken on time. Clarify directions before leaving the clinic.
2. Do NOT eat favorite foods during chemotherapy.
3. Pray without ceasing. Each day will come with new

blessings and new trials.
4. Pay attention to what works. Examples, Advil and Gatorade helped with the rigors. Keep in mind your own particular allergies and medication intolerances. Check with your oncologist before taking anything, including over-the-counter meds and even herbs.

Chapter 7: *No Piece Of Cake*

Approximately seven days after the first treatment, Howard started running a fever again. The thermometer read 103 degrees. The instructions were to call the doctor if it reached 100.5. The oncologist told me we had to go to the Emergency Room, because Howard probably was "neutropenic" (his bacteria-fighting white blood cells were deficient in number). I didn't know what that meant, but I was about to learn. I learned quickly, too, that I could not get through this without knowing God's presence. I talked to Him frequently.

After we arrived at the Emergency Room, they took several tubes of blood, a urine sample, and performed a chest X-ray. When Howard's blood pressure dropped, he broke out in a sweat, and he almost passed out. They told us Howard

might be "septicemic" (bacteria in the blood stream) and that he would be admitted to the hospital.
– From Beverley's Journal

In the emergency room, my blood pressure was initially very high. Then the fever spiked and I felt my blood pressure drop to nothing. I broke out in a sweat and slumped over on the gurney.

Those types of symptoms and signs usually mean septicemia, bacteria invading the blood stream due to diminished host immunity. But they never did find signs of infection. Nevertheless, I had to stay in the hospital until the fever was under control and my risk of septicemia was negated.

"I had a low point."

Late that night, well after Bev had gone home to rest and I had settled into my hospital room, I had a low point. I was sitting on the edge of the bed and waiting for a meal that I didn't really want. I just wanted to go home. I was weary and I rested my head on my hand—and came away with a clump of hair between my fingers.

Vanity, vanity. It hit me surprisingly hard.

I brushed away some tears and must have been sniffling a little, because I heard a voice behind me say, "Losing your hair, huh?"

I turned to see a visitor standing in the doorway. It was a tall, middle-aged man in a doctor's white lab coat; he had a sympathetic smile on his face.

"That really gets folks down," he said. "But it'll come back, you know. Maybe thicker than it was." This was a hematologist who was making rounds on behalf of the Cancer Center. An empathetic soul—one who would take over my care eventually, as my treatment progressed.

Lessons Learned

1. Be brave, but don't get cocky if you seem to fare better than the patient next to you. A little humility

never hurt anyone.
2. There are worse things than losing your hair.
3. It's okay to cry over losing your hair…or to cry because you feel like it.
4. But your hair *will* come back.

Chapter 8: *The Long Haul*

After five days of antibiotic IVs, Howard was released from the hospital with special instructions. He had to follow a neutropenic diet and precautions. That meant that he couldn't touch Daisy or clean up after her. He could not eat fresh raw fruits or vegetables; everything had to be cooked. When he was able to resume eating fresh fruits and vegetables, they had to be free of bruising or cuts where bacteria could grow. We had to be careful with dairy products, cheeses, and be sure they had no mold. We had already limited his sugar intake to keep his immune system up. He could not do any kind of yard work or handle potting mixes or plants. We had to avoid crowds, especially anyone that might be sick. When he did

"He had to follow a neutropenic diet and precautions."

return to work, he would wear a mask and gloves at all times. If anyone had the flu or the staph, in particular MRSA (Methicillin-resistent Staph Aureus), he would ask someone else to see the patient. We had to do whatever was necessary to keep from compromising his immune system.

> "We had to...keep from compromising his immune system."

Treatment number two went as scheduled, but about ten days after treatment he began to have uncontrollable shivering and a high fever again. Being a medical provider he was allowed to take medicine home and self-administer the shots, this time a new medicine called Neupogen, to himself in the abdomen. Later we found that by trial and error if the shots were given five days out from chemo, he would avoid being put in the hospital. He still got sick with extensive chills—what the medical community calls rigors—and some fever, but this allowed him to be at home instead of hospitalized. I would not leave the house unless I was sure he was okay. There were times when I was ready to take him to the ER, but he preferred to tough it out—over my objections—rather than risk more hospitalizations.

Most of his chemo treatments were given over the summer months, when it was incredibly hot, but Howard would bundle up in a t-shirt, sweatshirt, sweat pants and a hooded sweat jacket and I would find him standing in the 110 degree garage trying to get warm.

"...he rapidly started losing the rest of his hair."

After the second treatment, he rapidly started losing the rest of his hair. He stubbornly resisted the eventual outcome and he kept working with bald patches all over his head; he was leaving more hair on his pillow than was on his scalp. Even his eyebrows and eyelashes were disappearing. The oncologist admitted that though the type of lymphoma involved had a pretty good cure rate, it required a pretty tough course of chemotherapy and it was beginning to show.

Finally, I sat Howard down and told him of some female cancer patients I had met that just shaved their heads early in their treatments. He finally decided to get it over with.

We went out on the back patio and I took his electric razor and started to shave his head. I remember his wisps of fine hair blowing across the lawn in the breeze. It was very hard not to cry, but I tried to keep the mood light and so did Howard.

I bought him a fedora hat—what they call in Texas a Tom Landry hat—that he wore a few times before switching to a baseball cap. He went on to lose all his hair, even to the hairs in his nostrils.

He always maintained such a good outlook and a good sense of humor. There was a popular commercial on TV advertising Six Flags theme parks where an energetic senior citizen, bald and wearing big horn-rimmed glasses, was very agile and danced all over the place. They called him "Mr Six." Howard adopted the name and a few people at Howard's work started to call him Mr. Six. Whenever he would forget things, he also referred to himself as "chemo brain." The chemo brain phenomenon was a common discussion among the cancer patients—a sort of private joke, though it was a real enough problem.

When Howard was in the hospital I had to give Daisy, our yellow Labrador Retriever, the insulin shots she needed. My sister, who is diabetic, came from work to show me how to give the shots.

"...he also referred to himself as 'chemo brain.'"

I practiced sticking needles into oranges to get the feel of it. The insulin injections went well until I accidentally hurt Daisy and after that we would both get nervous. She was the sweetest dog I have ever had. The best disposition and she never attempted to bite anyone for any reason. She's my reason for hoping our pets go to heaven.

My family was wonderful during this time. I could call my sister-in-law at any time of day to go let Daisy out for me or to feed her if I could not get home in time. My youngest sister would come and give Daisy insulin shots when Howard and I had to be at the hospital.

"We learned what to do and what not to do..."

We learned what to do and what not to do to keep Howard strong during the treatments. Walking increased his white blood cell count. He would often require Procrit shots to increase his red blood count. I would give him raisins and molasses that are high in iron. I made him keep the sugar intake down as I believe sugar feeds the cancer and also lowers the immune system. Rest was very important because it would be restorative to the body.

I sat up in bed one morning and saw him stumbling down the hall toward me. He was trying to put a thermometer into his mouth, but couldn't because he was shaking so badly. He was wrapped in layers and layers of clothing and I immediately tried to get them off him. I constantly had to remind him that he was driving up the fever and though this was something he knew, he did it anyway. We tried all the remedies we so often used—Advil, Gatorade, forcing all kinds of fluids. We were supposed to go to the ER when he had fever over 100.5, but he would not go.

"*I never thought very far into the future...*"

I never thought very far into the future or ever considered that Howard, due to the cancer, might not be with me. Never knowing when the crisis of neutropenia would arise or other issues would strike, we took one hour, one day, one week at a time. All of my energy was used in taking care of him, making sure he had the right kind of foods to eat and preparing clothes that would be comfortable for him to wear. Every day was devoted to one thing: my husband's survival.

You have to remain flexible, because the day's plans change in an instant. We tried to do things that would keep our spirits up. Praying, listening to sermons, reading the Bible, and watching movies.

Howard loves Westerns, so we got a lot of these to watch. And lots of funny movies, because laughter is very good for the immune system...and because it would lift me up to hear him laugh. – From Beverley's Journal

Prednisone really pumped me up and gave me what seemed like heightened thought processes…at least, it provided me a hyper feeling. But along with that feeling came increased appetite and weight gain. Another patient on steroids told me that she felt like eating her own arm.

The Ups And Downs Of Steroids

The aftermath however, when the prednisone wore off, was the pits. I would get a rapid drop in energy, a rapid drop in my hemoglobin and platelets, and then would come the rigors and fever.

To combat the anemia, I took injections of Procrit to boost the hemoglobin. To forestall the neutropenia and promote bone marrow production to increase the neutrophil white cells needed to fight bacterial infection, I took injections of Neupogen. I received a drug called Neulasta initially, but it just didn't work for me and I always bottomed out with fever and low white count after my treatment. At least, Neupogen kept me out of the hospital. But again there was a price to pay.

While diminishing the rigors and fever, Neupogen introduced me to a whole new world of pain as my bone marrow revved up and, with every heartbeat, produced a deep throbbing in my sternum and in the base of my spine. The normal *lub-dub, lub-dub* of the heart became lub-BAM, lub-BAM in my chest. Fortunately, I only had to take the shots for eight days each three-week session.

"I envied them their ability to go home..."

In the chemo room, I used to lay back on my green recliner and watch the older patients shuffling by, carting their IV poles to and from restroom visits or to the nurse's station to chat and grab a free snack or a cup of coffee. I envied them their ability to go home after their chemo and rest until the next round of treatments. I was growing tired of tending to my own patients in my clinic while I felt like the walking dead myself. I suppose I indulged in a few pity parties, but I tried not to show that to anyone. I was supposed to be tough, brave, and mature while what I really wanted to do was go home and get under the covers and let Bev tend to me, God bless her. Poor Bev.

I wore a hat constantly by that time, mainly because my head was cold, but also to keep people from staring.

"There's a natural aversion to those who look different."

There's a natural aversion to those who look different. I did not much fancy looking at myself in the mirror. I saw a bald creature with a doughy complexion from tons of Prednisone looking back at me. My reflection reminded me of Uncle Fester from the Addams Family television show. Or perhaps that sprightly elderly spokesman for Six Flags: Mr. Six.

Intimacy

I read in cancer journals that some couples abandon each other physically and emotionally during this type of problem, especially if they're not blessed with spouses like Bev. Sex is okay between spouses during cancer treatment, generally, but not within two or three days of the chemotherapy treatment day. (Ask your doctor.)

It's okay to put your arm around a cancer patient's shoulder, although honestly, they probably won't appreciate someone offering to shake their hands due to their risk of infection. You can observe some veteran cancer patients using paper towels or cloth to open doors. (Germs on the door handles.)

A Time For Introspection

Anyhow, about this time, I started getting more and more philosophical, maybe a touch depressed. But I must say I learned a lot of scripture, things I never read before…or remember reading.

Why me?

We're all tempted to ask, "Why me?" But that's a question without an answer and it is self-defeating. Better to ask: *"To what purpose?"* If you insist on asking "Why me?" then you may as well ask the other side of that question: "Why did *I* survive when others did not?"

"To what purpose?"

Cancer is inconvenient. But you can give yourself a break, especially if, Lord forbid, you are going through this alone. You can let the laundry pile up more. You can leave the bed unmade when you're tired. You change your priorities quickly. Staying alive becomes number one. I tried keeping up with the lawn, at first, probably putting myself at risk, until I found my strength quickly ebbing. Mowing the lawn became a huge challenge and I gave it up, hiring someone to do it for me.

Taking chemotherapy during the summer, though, was a blessing. Since I am a health care provider, being immunocompromised during the flu season would have been horrendous. And winter weather would have been tough on me, because I was cold most of the time even in the summer.

Chemo Brain

My patients responded to me pretty well, even though I was wearing a mask, hat, and gloves. I think the kids were scared but the parents never pulled back.

I developed what's known among cancer patients as "chemo brain," a type of foggy thinking and maybe a little goofy behavior; however I was never considered an impaired provider and I made sure my treatments and medical records were accurate. (It's my opinion that chemo brain is due more to the steroids and stress than the chemotherapy drugs. But this is something that's being evaluated in chemo journals and oncology discussions.)

Pay attention to your symptoms and trust your instincts for survival. One time at work, I felt a slight chill and it concerned me. I checked my temperature, but it was only a mild 99.2. The doctor I mentioned it to, a co-worker, assured me that it was nothing to worry about. Later that night, I had a 103 fever and was hospitalized.

"Pay attention to your symptoms..."

Bev and I did what we could to aid the cancer treatments. Walking increased white cell production and therefore my immunity. Increasing fluids decreased my glucose levels and fought the cancer's predisposition to feasting on glucose. (The cancer has an affinity for glucose uptake, hence the uptake on a PET scan, which utilizes a glucose infusion before the scan.) Gatorade provided electrolytes.

Improving sleep improves the immune system. Lack of sleep, especially not getting to sleep before midnight, decreases your ability to fight infection and handle stress. Less sleep equals higher cortisol levels and increases adipose deposition. That's one reason that overweight folks should be getting more sleep, rather than less.

It's funny about neutropenia, because the "good things" become dangerous. Fresh fruit and vegetables had to be avoided when the neutrophils were low. Even when the neutrophil count was good, we were told to avoid multivitamins and other antioxidant medications within three days of receiving the chemo agents because they would block the agents' actions.

"...the 'good things' become dangerous."

During the days of chemotherapy, the world is upside down.

Lessons Learned

1. Stay close to God.
2. Stay away from sick people and animals.
3. Avoid shaking hands. Wash your hands often. Don't handle shopping carts, DVD rentals, etc.
4. Exercise (walking)
5. Get enough sleep, especially before midnight.
6. Remain flexible in your thinking, your planning, your responses to stress and schedules.

Chapter 9: *Crisis Mode*

We were doing well until about half way into the treatments.

A spot showed up during a routine PET scan done to check the progress of treatment. It was in the brain. One day we were on the home stretch, the next day we had appointments with a neurosurgeon and an oncology radiologist.

After MRI's, the neurosurgeon said that he felt it was the lymphoma affecting the brain and so they quickly scheduled Howard for a brain biopsy with the possibility of putting a port into his brain to receive chemo directly. There was also discussion of total brain radiation.

At the same time, we had more health concerns with our sweet dog Daisy. She had been diagnosed with Cushing's disease; her body producing too much cortisone (cortisol). The veterinarian started her on a medication considered to be a type of chemotherapy. Ironic. There were two chemo patients in the house, now.

> "There were two chemo patients in the house, now."

I had to keep a close watch on her. If she became real lethargic and non-responsive, I had to give her so many milligrams of Prednisone, the same medicine Howard had to take periodically. Daisy's appetite diminished and she became weaker by the day.

One afternoon, she would not move from her bed and would cry if we tried to pick her up. She finally got up but kept falling down and couldn't stand. After some dramatic soul-searching, Howard took her to the vet and she was admitted. (Howard had to do it. This was one thing I could not handle.)

Her diabetes was out of control and she would not eat at all. Our vet even went out and bought her some chicken but to no avail. Her kidneys started to fail. The vet tried to stabilize her sugar. He thought that it would be traumatic for Daisy to see us during her treatment. He also said that soon we would have to decide what course to take...which meant not allowing her to suffer, if things went badly.

"...I knew we would have to make a decision..."

Howard and I love animals and Daisy was part of our family, a wonderful companion, friend, and watchdog. Two days passed and I knew we would have to make a decision, one I dreaded. The only solution was to pray.

God cares about His creations and how they are treated and He answers and considers all prayers. You might ask why we were so concerned with Daisy while Howard was going through cancer treatments and facing the possibility of brain surgery. After 13 years of her presence in our lives, she was a good friend and she was family.

"She was a good friend and she was family."

The morning came when I knew we would have to call the vet, and I was on my knees in tears praying, "God please don't ask us to make this decision. Daisy is your creation and You should decide when her life is over." I begged Him to do what was best for Daisy.

An hour later we received a telephone call. Daisy had passed away.

She had a stroke and did not suffer, but I regret that we weren't able to say goodbye. Howard had the sad duty of going to pick up her collar.

Again, God had answered our prayers during a very difficult time, and He took on the burden when we could not. His Son told us, "Come unto me, all ye that labor and are heavy laden, and I will give you rest." Matthew 11:28

We didn't know what this brain surgery would do to Howard's mental alertness and there was the additional possibility of brain radiation. So, we started looking at options for our future. We looked at apartments for young seniors. We planned to sell our house and furniture, get rid of one car and do whatever needed to be done. We would be okay. God had always met our needs and very often met our wants.

> *"We started looking at options for our future."*

Without our faith we could not have gotten through this time. People let us down. But God would never fail. He wanted us to rely upon him and not on people. No, we did not plead for help or ask for comfort. If we had received visits and assistance from the Sunday School class (as, I admit, I expected and hoped for, and as was the custom in most churches), we would have put our focus on people rather than on God. He was and is our source of strength, our hope, and has supplied all that we need to take on the battle.

"He (God) was and is the source of our strength..."

Very often, cancer patients and families need help financially and churches can help. But help needs to be offered in tangible specific ways. We need to stay in touch and ask questions, be discerning and just help, if you sense the need. Write that check to your church instructing them to give the money to the family in need. Buy groceries,

make meals. Visit. Love and compassion will mend a heart and touch a soul. And maybe even stem the tide of cancer.
– From Beverley's Journal

On a follow-up PET scan in the end of July, they found a new mass in my brain.

The oncologist almost seemed to take it personally, not with so much empathy or sympathy, but with aggravation. He once told me that I'd never been a patient to do things the usual way. He set me up to see a neurosurgeon.

> *"...I decided that I had undervalued the need for compassion."*

It was at this time that I decided I had undervalued the need for compassion. Brains were good, but I needed a heart, too. I did not blame him, really, for feeling exasperated; I shared the sentiment. Nevertheless, I changed my attending oncologist to the hematologist that had checked on me in the hospital—the time my hair was first falling out.

Two weeks before my scheduled brain biopsy, Daisy began falling over. I took her to the vet while thinking I would never see her again. In the parking lot of the animal hospital, Daisy perked up and, right or wrong, like a coward I took her home again rather than into the hospital. It seemed like we had a second chance with her; it felt to me that it would be extremely stressful for her to be left alone in the vet hospital. It was a short reprieve.

"It seemed like we had a second chance with her..."

She had a seizure a few days later. I took her to the clinic again and this time I let them admit her. Bev's prayer, through her tears and sorrow, was to please don't ask us to take God's role in deciding Daisy's fate. Don't ask us to put her down. The next day, I received a phone call from the vet. He said that when they took Daisy for a little walk on the hospital grounds, she suffered a stroke and promptly passed away. Daisy was gone.

It looked like I had outlived Daisy, when I thought it would be the other way around. But I was not home yet.

My MRI findings suggested either a glioma or intracranial lymphoma, neither of which carried great prognoses.

Our next appointment would be with the radiation oncologist. Knowing that, and knowing what brain radiation would entail for me—a health professional, whose judgment and thinking had to be very clear—my wife and I began visiting local care facilities and low cost retirement communities.

While they had me in the OR, they would await an initial tissue analysis to determine whether I would emerge from the operating room with two holes in my head—one from the biopsy and the other from an intrathecal catheter that would allow intracranial chemotherapy. It sounded horrible, but you become accepting of the unacceptable when your life is on the line.

We visited Saint Francis Village, a small secluded neighborhood for the elderly run by Catholic Charities.

Wild turkeys roamed unmolested through the yards and there was a pleasant view of Lake Benbrook. It would be an idyllic low cost place for a brain-damaged cancer patient.

I smiled at Bev, though my heart was heavy. "Pretty nice out here. It won't be so bad."

But there was no room at the inn. Actually, there *was* room, but we were too young to meet their residents' criteria and by law, they could not accommodate us.

As if I did not have enough on my plate, it was during this period of time that I was due to sit for my national boards, the national certification that physician assistants have to take every six years. Great timing.

Let's just say that that was the fastest I had ever taken a four-hour board exam. I was in and out of the testing center under two hours. I actually passed with a decent score, despite my fatigue and chemo brain. I'm smarter than I thought…or I was more blessed than I realized.

Lessons Learned

1. God cares about all His creation—even our pets.
2. Be discerning about those suffering around you.
3. In the end, God will remain your strength.

Chapter 10: *Reprieve*

Howard's surgery was scheduled in August. We were to arrive at the hospital at 5:30 a.m. so that they could do a last MRI to check on the position of the brain lesion. Before we left for the hospital, I was on my knees before God and prayed that he would show His power and confound the wise.

Howard was taken to be prepped. As they put compression stockings on him and started an IV, I was instructed to withdraw to the surgical waiting room. My sister arrived with snacks, because this was to be a wait of about four hours depending on what the pathology report revealed. My sister-in-law was on her way to join us.

We had just settled in the waiting room when the neurosurgeon came in and told me they were sending Howard home. My first thought was that they had already gone in and the lesions were benign. The doctor said that after looking at the MRI that morning, they noted that the previous lesion was gone. I started to cry, while my sister just sat there with her mouth open.

We had just received a miracle from God. Howard was released and those in the pre-op room said they had never seen that happen before. People may leave because something wasn't right for the surgery to go forward, like an abnormal EKG, etc., but this reason was very unusual. This day, our God confounded the wise, the doctors and all the staff, and He showed His mighty power. God is in control. – From Beverley's Journal

On August 27, the morning of my scheduled brain biopsy, the neurosurgeon had me undergo a final MRI of the brain. That done, I was admitted to the hospital and taken to the pre op area. I had surgical stockings put on and had the traditional visit by the anesthesiologist who started the IV while he explained the procedures to me.

I was lying there (my wife having departed to the waiting room), when the neurosurgeon approached and looked down at me. "I can't operate on you." He continued to stare at me as if I were a strange specimen.

"Why not?"

"Because your brain lesion is gone," he said.

"Gone?"

"The brain lesion we discussed is absent. You have a new one, down in the brainstem. I think you're having small strokes from migraines. I believe you have a history of them. I'm going to have you see a neurologist about the migraines. You can go ahead and get dressed." No smiles. No congratulations. He was gone.

I lay there a minute, stunned. What a rare thing, getting dressed and walking out of the operating room. Feeling a trifle guilty, I watched all the other patients being wheeled to the operating suites.

Into my pre-op cubicle rushed my wife, ecstatic and grinning, with her sister literally jumping up and down with joy beside her.

"I'm going home," I said. *And, I added silently, without holes drilled into my head and without having to have total brain radiation and without having my thinking and memory go foggy.* I watched more patients carted out toward surgery as I got dressed. I got a few stares from the nurses and attendants. I guess the oncologist was right; nothing typical about my case…right down to the wire.

Lessons Learned

1. God answers prayers and confounds the wise.
2. God is faithful.
3. It's not over until God says it's over.
4. Every day is a gift from God.

Afterword

From Bev

Much is said, these days, about maintaining a positive attitude. Important, yes. But even more important is staying close to God…in prayer, in your thoughts, when you're troubled, even when you're angry.

When my mother was sick with cancer, before the availability of FMLA, I took an unpaid leave of absence to be with her. I didn't know at the time that that would be the last two weeks of her life. Those were precious times…every moment. I cared for her until my dad and siblings got home from work. The roles changed between my Mom and me. I felt I was the parent and she the child.

I bathed her and combed her hair. I stayed with her at her home, so she would not have to remain in the hospital. You'll never regret the time you spend with loved ones and friends in such times.

Caregiving can be short-term, long-term or lifelong. God does not call the equipped, he equips the called. I believe He does that for everything we face in our lives. He equips us and is with us. To some, caregiving doesn't come naturally, to others it's second nature, but even so, we all need refreshment. We all need help and encouragement. Sometimes that comes from others, but most of the time it comes from God.

From Howard

My final (I hope) chemotherapy treatment was completed, without incident, 21 months ago. Minus my gallbladder, appendix, and a little piece of my liver, I still get to keep my brain intact (such as it is after a lifetime of migraines and, apparently, mini-strokes). And I am alive. I am blessed and I know it. We'll see how my follow-up PET scan does in August this year, but I am a cancer survivor, because I am still here with you.

Did this experience result in a whole new Howard? I don't know…that's a tough one. I certainly have a greater, deeper appreciation for being here, for just being alive, for being here on earth to love and provide for my wife and my family.

But I cannot forget fellow travelers who did not finish this earthly journey with me and I would like to mention them.

There was a psychologist—a gentle soul I knew from the university—who stopped in the oncology clinic while my wife and I were waiting to see my doctor. The psychologist was recently diagnosed with multiple myeloma, a painful cancer that attacks the bones. He sat down beside us and spoke with us. He was alone, his wife a busy physician in her own right, but I could tell he was apprehensive and he appreciated our speaking with him and praying openly for him, though, clearly, I had my own troubles.

There was Mrs. M., a mother of twelve children. She was a patient of mine who eventually succumbed to breast cancer. She was one of the bravest people I've ever known and her children were the sweetest kids. One of her boys, last time I met them at my clinic, gave me a little gift—a folded origami dove with the words "Holy Spirit" written on its wings. That was when I was going through chemo and feeling sorry for myself.

There was my boss' daughter, a feisty, courageous young woman with breast cancer. There was a co-worker's sister, another young woman who valiantly fought brain cancer. And there was my friend, Rick. All brave, decent people.

But there are survivors too; many survivors who—only God knows why—are still here. God willing, you or your loved one will be among them, should you be struggling with cancer.

Remember the lady who shouted out at me while having her reaction to chemo on my first day of treatment? I've seen her since—one time, in fact, sitting right next to me as we both waited for the port flushes we have to have every eight weeks. Her hair was brown and curly, her flesh pink and amply padding her once bony frame, and the color was back in her cheeks. There are others, many others, who do quite well and go back to their full, precious lives.

I don't know why some go on, and some don't. I don't know why children get cancer or good people suffer.

There will be some dark moments for the one with cancer. Lonely moments. But they are not all bad.

There will be a time in which God raises the cancer patient to a higher relationship with Him, One-on-one. It will be an intimate path, unlit and narrow, down which the patient will be led by Him, one step at a time…that is, if the patient is open to this solemn, sometimes scary, introspection and listening.

As for you and I…maybe we're here to help others along the way, if nothing more than with a joke and a chuckle, a hug, a bucket of chicken, and a prayer. The way Rick joked with me and prayed for me—even from his death bed. The way Rick was concerned for me, a fellow traveler.

Appendix A
Quick Reference: Survival Tips

1. **FMLA:** (if employed by a company) file paperwork under the Family Medical Leave Act as soon as you know you have to have prolonged cancer treatment.
2. **Facility Location:** choose a good cancer treatment facility that is close to home. You will be making many trips back and forth.
3. **Clothing:** wear loose, comfortable clothing for chemo treatments and procedures. (Jogging suits are good.) Allow for access to your port-a-cath, if you have one.
4. **Nausea:** non-prescription products: ginger ale (the ginger is an anti-emetic), peppermint, Emetrol, soda crackers.
5. **Mouth ulcers:** non-prescription products for mouth ulcers: Colgate Orabase (topical cream), Zilactin (reddish liquid, strong smell, but forms nice coat on ulcer).
6. **Pain:** Advil or Motrin (Ibuprofen) is effective for

mild to moderate pain and fever. Avoid if you have diminished renal (kidney) function. Tylenol (Acetaminophen) was not recommended by our cancer physicians, possibly due to more toxic liver effects. Best to ask your physician about this tip.

7. **Reactions versus septicemia:** Both can cause fever and chills. Don't try to guess—call your oncologist for significant fever (100.5).

8. **Insurance:** be sure that all your medical providers have current copies of your insurance. If you are fortunate enough to have two medical insurance coverages, as in Blue Cross *and* Medicaid, for example, then ensure the providers have copies of both. What one insurance does not completely cover, the other will likely take up.

9. **Travel bag:** have a bag handy for unexpected hospital admissions. Include toiletry, Chap Stick, mints, change of clothes, etc.

10. **Lunch box:** inexpensive food carrier for snacks, drinks.

11. **Diet:** Eat as tolerated during chemo, but the rule is to not crowd your stomach. **Avoid favorite foods** during your entire chemotherapy period (from first to last chemo treatments). You may develop lasting intolerance for foods by associating them later with chemo-induced nausea. Avoid sugar/sweets. Some cancer cells have an affinity for glucose. Maintain good hydration.
12. **Sleep:** Get at least eight hours a day and try to get to bed well before midnight. Sleep after midnight is less beneficial. Lack of sleep increases stress and unwanted weight gain.
13. **Exercise:** walking, stretching, deep breaths. Exercise will boost your white count and relieve stress. A recent study suggests periodically sighing or taking a deep breath boosts the immune system.
14. **Loss of hair:** not much you can do to prevent it. Wear a hat, buy a wig, or go natural. You (and those around you) will get over the initial strangeness. For some guys, it's an improvement!

15. **Faith:** Don't lose it. Hang onto it. Pray and share your concerns with God and with intimate friends and family.

Appendix B
Neutropenic Diet & Precautions

1. Assume you are neutropenic (low white blood cell count) if you are febrile (running a **fever**).
2. **Avoid:**
    Fresh salad

    Fresh, raw vegetables

    Unpeeled fruit

    Dried fruit

    Raw nuts

    Nuts in shells

    Pepper (yes, pepper from shakers)

    Uncooked chili pepper

    Cheese from deli

    Bakery bread, muffins

    Potato salad

    Macaroni Salad

    Any raw or undercooked meat

    Deli meats, salami

    Oysters

(**Avoid,** continued)

Well water or water from a spring

Egg nog

Sun tea

Homemade lemonade

Fresh salad dressing

Cream- or custard-filled donut

Raw honey

Brewers yeast

3. **Do not handle:** pets or pet cages/beds/clothes, bird cages, plants, grass/lawn cuttings, potted soil (any soil, for that matter), grocery cart handles, door knobs, DVD cases or anything handled by others.

Microwave machines may not thoroughly cook food. (Frequently turn microwave food to ensure cooking.) Disinfect tops of cans before opening and disinfect can openers after use. **This is a partial list. Your cancer center should provide detailed neutropenia information.**

Appendix C
Helpful Resources

1. CancerCare (www.cancercare.org)
   Includes CancerCare For Kids, free counseling

2. Caring4Cancer (www.caring4cancer.com)
   Offers individual online patient health record and "symptom tracker"

3. Heal (www.healtoday.com)
   Emphasis on cancer survivors

4. Mamm (www.mamm.com)
   Dedicated to serving women with breast and gynecological cancers

About the Authors

Howard Clarke is a cancer survivor. He is the author of software programs, medical articles, and "Divine Dialogue," a gift book about familiar Biblical phrases. He is an assistant professor at a medical university and, as a Physician Assistant, attends to Family Medicine patients. He is working, currently, on a novel.

Beverley Clarke is co-author of "When Cancer Comes Your Way," her first publication. Beverley is involved in Christian-Jewish charities, in particular Bridges of Peace, a charity group that feeds impoverished Jewish and Arab families in the Holy Land, and Zola Levitt Ministries.

Howard and Beverley live in Fort Worth, Texas. Daisy, their yellow Lab, lives in their memories.

www.howardfclarke.com